bourgess

collection se

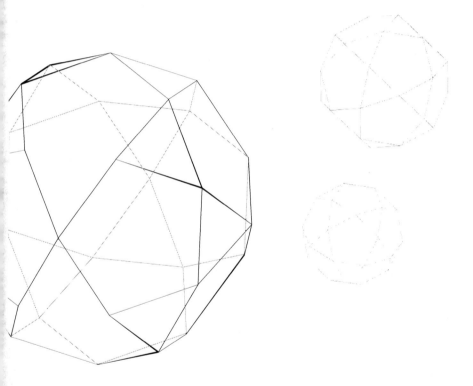

Burch Rockwell Driver

Bourgess
Special Edition

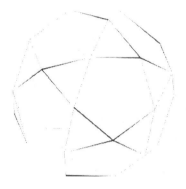

Introduction

Everyone walks their own path, but all who seek
find themselves in the same place. In the finding,
we realize there was never any path to take. These
poems are the witnessing of the cross sections of
awareness. Like three-dimensional cards, each
moment is a singular slice of an infinite
assembly. The world moves past our eyes though we
imagine that we move past the world. The strobing
aspect of experience becomes continuous when we
recognize the incompleteness of our perspective.
It is but flashes in the pan. We all have to be
our own helping hand in the darkness. Doing so is
not transcendence because that objective is only a
measurement from a limited viewpoint. Being
unlimited is the recognition that what we see is
an interface, both the perception apparatus and
the externalities are one thing. To force a
separation is the forever start again at the
beginning. We can transcend though as a collective
with an immeasurable mindset. There is nothing to
be done except remember. Then we assemble and the
sky is the literal limit. Enjoy!

Part I

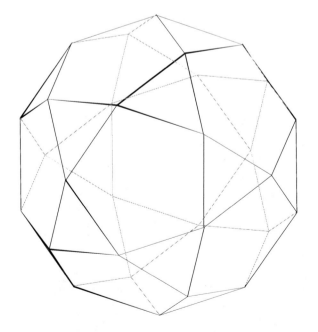

The way

The way
is not
the middle
when you
think it such
one side
or the other
is as much
when considered
correct
is it you who decides
to make it
better
when engaged
in creative endeavor
it will be done
when you let it

The present

The present
not an event
in the mind
thought
an illusion of time
presence has no units
no derivative
its rate of change
is nil and infinite
no starting and
no stopping
no soft hands
or dropped passes
no classes
or conversations
can remove the glasses
of condition
cause one to awaken
oh, how quickly
you arrive
when there is
no path to be
taken

Imaginary

I'll shut down
the conversation
because it's boring
a circle on a plane
drawn with a
borrowed compass
I'll stop you before
you reach the second
quadrant
then I open up the
hydrant
I'm justified
like Timothy Oliphant
except tall
and non-lethal
hydro scaling your
misconception
I'm not interested in
a revolution
only the solution
it isn't complex
it's simple
transcendental
the unseen component
natural log raised
to an imaginary exponent
times Pi
plus one
equals zero
turns out we are
all the hero
but not the standard
bearer dying
on the hill
riddled with arrows
there is nothing to
fight or protect
throw down your
arms so we can
assemble the project

Novelty

Does it happen
or is it done
how many
forks in the
road taken
to arrive
at the outcome
Is it freewill
or predetermined?
the combined total
of individual choosing
Leads to
periodicity of
collective destiny
and that's just irony
selecting
choicelessness
though
leads to
novelty

Fair play

It is fair
life
the balance
is never left
out of line
it comes
eventually
to step
in step
with the
rhythm
maintains
the equilibrium
not
waiting
for the
echo
she speaks
directly
without reflection
the delay
is in the replay

The center

Be done?
you can't
if from
a perspective
that is
measured
you are not
small
the distance
from
your skin
to the scale
of within
is proportional
to the
optical range
of the James Webb
even more
strange
the center
is
wherever
you look
from
now you're
done

Face up

Every second
is a card
face up
or down
to the
unknown
pull
one out
or
put it back
in
the new is
drawn
the old
discarded
there are infinite hands
but
we insist
on a short
deck

The message

Have you seen
the movie
The Red Violin?
not a viola
or a cello
or a bass

a violin
with a particular
sound

the color
made it identifiable
yet its chromatic
scale
was the
signature
an object that
by specific
manipulation
offers a
cross-section of
creation

ah ha!
exclaims McLuhan
the message
is
the medium

Spinning

In the open
outside the closed
unbounded
but
finite
containing
an origin
without a
localization
angular
momentum
increases
with
radius
But where
is the center?
corresponding
to a previous
state of matter
the hub
location of the
apparatus
cannot
be
seen
with your eyes
it is
your eyes

Three

One cannot
see it
hear it
or hold it
but
one can receive
it
fruition
with
whole
perception
when
one are three
the invisible
inaudible
and
intangible
become
available

Lagrange

There is
a place at the end
called the beginning
where the behind
ends and
the front
begins
the threshold
of the time
between
times that
are noted
as start
and restart
rise
and set
would that I could
rest there
in the null transitions
temporary
Lagrange

Contrast

Contrast
the difference
of background
relative to the
fore
before and
after
clear
demarcation
up
and
down
the well
left and right
of center
thing
and
nothing
observed
all of these
indicate
difference
but each
allows
the others'
existence

Automatic

Nature runs on
automatic
for all time
you have to wonder
though
Who turned it
on?
it grows
seems as
if there was
a beginning
because we
can observe
incremental
density
thinning
something
started
but
What came first?
the breath out
or the breath in

Portal

I opened the door
the difference
was clear
between inside
and out here
to my senses
no need to
explain why
but isn't it interesting
to try

the heat
the energy of
yesterday
slowly dissipated
through the pains
and cracks
the edges of the
portal

but it was
palpable
the difference
still
less molecular
movement
until later
when the sun
imparts energetic
wisdom to the
atmospheric solution

Maw

Casting a long shadow
requires a low
light
in between
the time
between
on that history
the sun has set
as the darkness dissolves
into light
all the love you gave
poured into
the maw
all that love
is not gone
but rises

Delineation

From thin air
out of it
comes form
Aether ̄
Emanates,
light illuminates
shadow delineates
concentrates
awareness

Reminders

Walking in the dark
extrasensory attempts
met with reminders
compulsory course corrections
navigation by reaction

pre-emanation
sans prescient
preemptive
underinformed
vision is prediction

in the dark unseen
obstacles imply passage
progress can be measured
by touch
over, around, through

in the light, the way
cannot be found
if there is nothing
to go around

Reversal

If there was
a future
then that is
a reversal
of the direction
of time
and therefore, the past.

if there is
a future
it is
speculation

Parallel

A plane, infinite
parallel
will not touch
another
is only itself
with dimension
out
back
or in

complexity is a
mental space
so I stop thinking

Inside the out

Does that stop
where this begins?
How far down
do you go
before
rising again?
Do you step out
from within?
or
Are you without
the in when
inside the out?
it's tricky
sometimes to figure
where you are
and the rest is not
or is it that you
forgot
to remember and
remembered to
breath in
breath in
breath out
begin
end
again

Relative

After implies a before
self-realization is
recognizing what is
always here
now is the beginning
and the end
relationship
with acausal intent
is wise action
without gauging
relative
not automatic but
choiceless
choice is separate
divided, dual, independent
the ever-present
is
interdependent
indivisible
immeasurable
selfless

POV

Point of view is divided
subjective
pure awareness
accepts
the rejection
of
personal perspective
seeing from there
is objective

Holding

Machiavelli once said:
There is no sure way
of holding
another
than by
destroying.

Surely that is
a guarantee that
you will be held in turn
subject to the effect
of artificial rhythm
but
accepting uncertainty
is the return
the
superposition of
momentum
and
position.

Remember

From the womb
there
is no choice
no action
can actively
be taken
it all happens
of it own
volition

breathe
the shocking
introduction

a miracle
but only one
of millions
let us add
just one more
it's a big ask
considering
what should be
VS
what we've been doing

let us remember

Alignment

If alignment
is
two lines
that never
meet
it is
two
planes
that never
intersect
a measurable separation
but
to cross
paths
intersect
is interference
a disturbance
a singular agitation
from which emanates
a wave
not a line

Cartesian

The three
spatial
dimensions
the origin
cartesian
planar
intersection
arbitrary
reference point
to begin
counting from
counting in units
equal segments
of a line
or a vector
a direction
a magnitude

Signal

The signal has been sent
silence
tick tock goes the sky clock
while the trees wait

Terrain

Difficult terrain
precise navigation of
some would call it grace

Ever

Ever-present
background
sound
a humming
inaudible
yet palpable
nonlocal
strings
resonating
my
heart

Still

The boat rocks
gently
the water is calm
to the eye
but the subtle
movement
tilts the vessel
this way
and that
the nudge
the lap
on the hull
transmissions
tiny disturbances
sent
yet
received
only when the mind
is still

Running

I sat down to
write
about nature
mountains
trees and
rocks
and streams
but was drawn
to consider
people
and
why is that
they
do not
seem natural
Is it because
nature runs
itself
on automatic?
while we
while we
make choices
But who
is running
our hearts?

Happening

It can happen
the stone is not
set
fixed
it was refused
but awaits
your hands
for placement
prepare
with
proper alignment
the wall
of the garden
the cornerstone
of your soul

Pressure

I go
out
into nature
looking at the ground
the detritus
it is
I observe
thousands upon thousands
of layers
each pressed
down by
the last
only the top one
the specks of dust,
smoke
the air
presses
itself

Subject

What is an object?
can we say
it is a thing
existing
in time
and at a place
an event
yet sustained
How does it come
into being?
the result
of a chain,
a sequence,
a culmination
objects follow
the subject
an idea
an object is a subject
of awareness
and arrives
when finally regarded

Dreaming

If you say
you had a dream
it can mean two things
the kind you have
while sleeping
or the kind you give up on

Rheostat

The lights are flickering
at my Dad's house
it is likely
the old rheostat
the Gen X wiring
can't help thinking though
perhaps it's my father
still inhabiting
why
my mind betrays me
the motivation
of a ghost

Torrent

I am numb
except for when I'm not
I am numb
except I feel more than ever
breaking through my jade wall
I am indifferent
except when I crack open
let the flood wash over me
it feels comforting
in those raging waters
it is easy to navigate
let go
it feels so good
to let my foot fall off the break
shut my eyes and
drop by hands from the wheel
and let the torrent
run its course

Blessings

The rain begins
again
it's unprecedented
in the high desert
I can feel
others
marveling and discussing
the oddity of it
but
there is a
superposition in their
minds
and
my own
a fluke
a blip in the trend
or an indication
despite my misgivings
I feel
we are in for more
blessings

Grow

You grow up
thinking
they are the stuff of legends
in stories
they show up for heroes
and in tragic comedies
oracles
and prophecy
whether by divine intervention
or self-fulfilled
they are that
in any case
signs and portents

Gradation

I like gradation
the smooth transition
I like atmospheric perspective
the depth of volume
otherwise unseen
at noon or under the new moon
stark contrast
I also like
but not the blast of a horn
or the snap of a flood tripped by a sensor
I like sharp shadows
made by the sun
cast overlapping
on a liquid surface
but
a shadow grows
and shrinks gradually
I suppose
I prefer
that kind
of
change
the foliage
on the fan
of a mountain
rising to the rocky passes
I could name a thousand
such things

Picaris

Going to an area
south of here
will bring you to
a mountain
older than
before
before, there were mountains here
worn down to
nothing
by weather
before that
even
there was a lonely mountain
rising to heaven

Mist

I long for the
past
of my previous
lives
despite knowing
the reverberations
of long stilled
suffering
I miss
the mist
on the moor
seen from a rise
with standing stones

Meta

Speeding through the desert
approaching
mountains with details
I've never imagined
I catch a glimpse
of a tie bridge
spanning a wash
and
I think
oooh there's some history
in the dirt and the sunbaked rocks
meta past
witnessed
and
near the river
while entering the
mysterious mountains
containing the flowing border
suddenly an island
of tightly packed mobile homes
with boat docks

Locomotive

The big questions
come into my view
often when looking at small things
not small
just not cosmic
.like seeing
a freight train
just after sunset
while going 90 across the desert
an impossibly long line
of box cars
suddenly ending

Blinkers

The outcome
destiny
is an inversion
choosing guarantees
your location
while surrender
allows for variation
you've been hoodwinked
accepted the blinkers
following the carrot
making ruts
that form a circle

Looking

looking around
with eyes that see
the rocks,
trees,
the stream
all looking back at me
not you though
you're fucking blind

Fate

Up the mountain
there is completion
keep climbing
that's what they
say anyway
for me, I have
doubts
that the end,
the point at which
you can
no longer ascend
the destination
is destiny
that word is romantic
sounds better maybe
because it's a choice
to climb
and say you did it
destiny though
is an ending we can
avoid
while fate
fate
must take
place

Market

It is strange
Is it not?
queer
that we find ourselves here
wonderful and curious
and yet
we all forget
and fresh, unmarked
immediately branded
and fattened for market

Ways

Four ways to play
five ways
to feel
uncounted
roll of the dice
again
again
again
your soul
again
your body
again
your heart
again
your mind

Grace

Grace is not
for the win
or to lose
only to
take the next step
the next best step
there is a way
through

Humility

Do not boast
lest you get roasted
do not brag
or be red flagged
but
roast your self
and be toasted
raise your flags high
and wave
to be thought brave
either way, it's done for effect
do or do not say it
I am humble
I am meek
that is the right way to be
naw,
that's not humility

Bukowski

He was brilliant
his pain sold books
to maintain
he drank
like wearing sunglasses
dependent upon the filter
the polarized lens
of the tumbler
and bourbon
permitted him to see
the page
without being
blinded
by the light of his soul

Part II

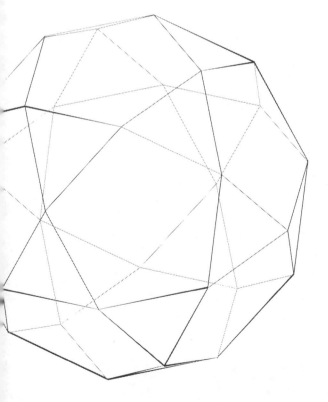

Elevated

An elevated
point
looking down
from above
with no water
in the sky
offers the long view
the desert
is different like that
territories
vistas
and the mystery
down in the valleys
canyons
a sense that
something has happened
in these lands

Why

It is okay
to let go
to surrender
to the unknown
every moment
is
the little death
and rebirth
is
the next
but that is only part
of what the
old masters suggest
it is to put
your whole and entire
sense of your separate self
to rest
it is dead already
because it exists
in the past
It consists
of
experience and memory those
crumbling walls
and faded images
require constant repair
don't spend the rest
of
your life
maintaining
what isn't there
it only persists
in your mind
because you insist
that it is
you
It's full-time
preoccupation
meanwhile the future
has already left the station
forget how and what and why
you are trying to be
your memory
come with me

Memory

My words
are
water
dripping
in the back of the cave
layered mineral memory
drip drop drip
10,000 years
and
still sleeping

Wall

Certain memories
are clear
it seems
but the review
in your mind
of
that one time
recalls the
color
the texture
of the wall
but much less
the faces
that were there
more, it's feeling
that populates
the spaces
of the past

Back then

When you think
of
the image of life
in a time
long past
everyday
you see something
made
back then
it's fascinating
and sad
the remnants
I want there to be more
than remembering
though
more than the broken
parts
of an old assembly

Leftovers

Reheat the past
ashes are umami
I declare
taste best
when sprinkled with despair
hope
the desert isn't better
then a cocktail
with a splash of bitters

Not kidding

I'm interested in the
grand collaboration
it's cliche´ though
so, I'm hesitant to say
I'm kidding
I don't give a fuck
let's design our culture
not to suck

Once

Suddenly
that's how it comes
the realization
it doesn't fade
after
but glows
asking to be used
deployed
rolled out
but
we mostly
just shelf it
and look at it
once in a while

Project

What is the objective?
he asked
for this project
to be completed
The object is to complete
the project?
yes,
to name all the things
and their locations
classify all types
and categorizations
How does this help
you?
to know
where to go
and what to do
When?

Sole

A compelling
sounds like
a horror movie
or a tale
of the supernatural
the first colony
the sole survivor
from Roanoke
Island
but it's the quality
of an argument
a statement
in a debate
or a piece of art
a poem
or photograph
something
that invokes
or evokes
action

Music

A thousand crickets
in the night, sounds like music
one, is deafening

Weapon

They thought it couldn't
be done
to be creative
at the barrel of a gun
but what they didn't know
and what they will find
is that
the weapon is the mind

0-2

Like you
I'm divisible
when I'm tired
the razors edge
is so fine
when asking
in the asking voice
the way becomes
a wire
frayed balance
slack
when something is
lacking
but
remember
when you
previously
got that second wind
2 nil down
and came back
to win?

Sometimes

Sometimes
the little things
the inconsequential
the superfluous
the way the
pieces won't
fit
but they do
and somehow its
you
your state
the distraction
of the wait
does not permit
the key
to enter the lock
the zipper
to be zipped
the coffee filter
seated
make you aware
that you
do
care

Good

Not much surprises
me anymore
but I just knocked on wood
you know
because despite
the nonchalance
I show
I'd prefer a good surprise
this time

Uncommon

All of these
gifts I was born
with
are a letter
in a bottle
sent adrift
a dandelion
seed
floating this way
and that
on the breeze
bumping the hull
of a larger vessel
not uncommon
in the field
I wrote that message
I made that wish
my fate
is sealed

Action

I filmed myself
with an action cam
writing a poem
the image stabilization
software
was not tested
all the
movement
was
inside

See

I'm a member
of a group
an FB community
I have to wonder
if it's real
or if the people are
I haven't witnessed
any transformations
so far
this group, its
spiritual,
nondual,
and virtual
intangible
I pop in
once in a while
to drop bombs
rattle some cages
I do it with
impunity
a kind of diplomatic
immunity
because all I get
are crickets
it's rare
when someone
engages
one time though
I made a connection
we met eyes
in the dark of the internet
passing with a nod
to knowing
then they were gone
an interesting catch 22
we do
I see you
I see you too

Nothing

Teachers of the truth
who offer it for free
are regarded suspiciously
but, when a partial truth in a package
is given for a fee
we pay willingly
surely everyone is perfect
as they are
that's not irony
the truth is though
they look externally
convinced of a problem
and a solution to buy
but who is forcing
if not the one who is
choosing
only when
there is nothing wrong
is there space for improving
certainly, words are a trap
but it's what we have
and so I yell if only
to tell
you...
there is no path
to the truth
it's inside you

Novelty

My name is my name is Burch
I have been trying to reach you
every generation
I speak to everyone
but the boomers, they are out of time
to make a quality contribution.
this is a reintroduction
so you have some context
I am for something different
and I wouldn't,
I absolutely would not do this
if what I have
wasn't a furnace
I share to bleed off the pressure
hear me out
so I can drop my temperature

or run away
weak links will break
go ahead then
we need the real
not the fake

I'm uncomfortable
there is something wrong
I'm fine
my body and my mind are strong
but my spirit is screaming
we're running out of time

I'm uncomfortable
I'm about to make you that way
because comfort is dangerous ideologically
resting in your identity divot
is fragile
transformation
is the ability to pivot
on a dime
meditating, fasting, and ice-cold water
won't get you there in time

this is for the spirit
spiritual instruction
Can you handle it?
or are you part of the problem?

go away if you have to
weak links break
go ahead
we need real
not fake

so here it is then
the transformation that we need to make
its collective
but there is no adjustment
to the system
that will be effective
we look outside using our intellect
but inside each of us
is the cause of the defect
we treat the symptoms and ignore
the root problem
we are all culpable

now you're uncomfortable
fuck you, you say
I can vote
I recycle drive a prius or a tesla
bring my own bag to shop for groceries
text my bestie and my lithium battery
heats up my testes or my ovaries
see the irony, the hypocrisy?

run away if you must
weak links break
go ahead, we need real
not fake

so what is it then?
you ask with anger rising
it's so fucking simple
it might be surprising to you
but you need the complex

so you can defer to the experts
that's your reflex
Who are you to say?
What is your degree in?
How much do you get paid?
that's it right there. you just indicated
the reprobated material property
credibility is all about popularity
the mainstream won't let the truth reach
anyone on livestream it comes in disguise
i walk right up to you in camouflage
but you can't see anything without a package
do you get it yet
followership is manufactured
you miss all the messages not coming from our
sponsors

share and like this till the algorithm gives
in
it's trained to show posts
that promote division

gen x rappers dissing you
are they really that slow?
it's been how long, and they still haven't
caught on?
naw, they're just working for the man
acting sold out, playing a role
just like you though
brother
they show up in your feed
and you eat it up though
sister

we can't fix the system
with the system
that's the clue
it's what I'm teaching you
there is a better way
it's not supposed to be pay-to-play
value comes from living
not a limited supply supplier
fuck those guys

we want the statistical outlier
unpredictable aberration
unidentified operator
additional value generator
Lorentzian attractor
value redistributor
which can never arrive
from inside
the credibility hive
to break the cycle means
recognition of value
without sponsorship
the ability to support novel authorship
the courage to jump ship
to a worthy vessel
and turn on your gifts on to
maximum output level

What is the instruction?
abandon belief reject conditioning
forego identity embrace doubt
to make space for the pursuit of knowledge
but not the kind you get at college
your transformation comes with the
realization
that it isn't about you or your
manifestations
your legacy or intentions
we only avoid the limit
of our behavior by coming together
humanity transcends as a unit
or it doesn't do it
if you can wake up for real
you will be able to feel
the nudge
activate whole perception
and permit wise action
only then can we operate in co-creation
creating an organization
immune to corruption
if you can't comprehend this
you're controlled opposition
hamstrung by your belief

that our problem is our nature
and not our condition

that's why I'm here
that's my mission
to break the pattern and restore balance
to our civilization
Are you with me?
or do you think it will replay
and we'll all wake up again
to another groundhog day?

As I said

I am working on a big project
it is the seemingly impossible
a positive outcome
for us all
you may see this as hubris
or more likely, foolish
what is the use of attempting this?
maybe, I am a fool
perpetually evaluating what is useful
is more practical
identifying what is to be discarded
so the suitable can be completed
is competent
more efficient
right?
but, qualifying the advantages is still
ongoing
doing the profitable is as of yet
insufficient
How long have we been at it?
the pragmatic
endless measurement
Which then is more feasible?
I say
the impossible
is the only outcome that is
achievable
because the alternative is never ends
the miraculous happens
when there is nothing to be done
or to be chosen
if the observer
and the observed
are in superposition

Part III

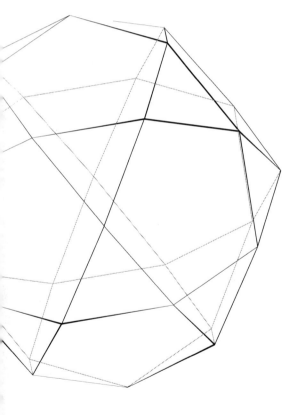

Disturbance

Everyone says
alignment is the objective
but by definition
alignment is two lines
that can never meet
it's
two surfaces that never
intersect
everyone says alignment is good
ideal even
but I don't want it
I want to cross paths
I want to meet up
I want to intersect
I want to interfere
I want to be a disturbance
to you

Ones and zeros

I have never seen her
not with my eyes
only reassembled bits
ones and zeros
yeses and nos
open and closed
gates
times one trillion
built-up
by a device
and yet
we have met before
held hands and laughed
with our feet in the grass
on a higher plane
one time
briefly
in the distant past

Indelible

Time dependency
temporal
patience everlasting
temperance
duration in the fire
transient
pressure
temper
temperature of passion
limited action
temporary passing
impossible solute
imperishable quench
eternal flame
indelible

Citadel

The path to
the citadel
thorns
brambles
false divergence
washouts
fallen rock
unpassable
no trace
and yet
and yet
suddenly a ladder
in the stone
acclivity aperture
then
a spanning viaduct
afforded
essential
impossible
ingress

Furnished

To clear the air
not thin it
invert space
time
bank it
assemble words
tasked
presented with
challenge
my cherished pass-time
obstinance notwithstanding
my own
likely the test
I leave incomplete
retired
firm standing
I cannot see
in the dark
yet walk
furnished halls
unlit
to be near you

Void

This wonderful
void
evacuated bell
this exquisite ringing
excited
nothingness
astonishing
differential pressure
potential difference
electrifies me
the incandescence of my being
I bleed off
incrementally
with these words
shrouded in steel
lest I burn
down
the
sky

Sharpy

I write this in sharpy
so the intent
is not lost
I put it in **bold**
so it's hot
no question
like HD
high fidelity
gas on a fire
I want to light you up
and
see your little
sun
beat like a drum

Noises

Sometimes a noise
a scooting of a chair in class
the click of a latch
the squeak of the floorboards above you
the sound of forced air kicking on
at 4 AM
you notice them
these disturbances
the pop of the fire
the magnetic strip on the fridge
but
Can you hear the blink of my eyes
when I turn to look at you?
the movement of my fingers
the instant at which I begin to breathe in
after breathing out
Can you hear it?

Alone

I like the cold
it makes me feel warm
I like high-altitude
if I make the climb
I like being alone
sometimes in a crowd
I like the stage
but not so much conversation
I like to learn
to destroy preconception
I like to walk in the dark
where the light is my memory
I like to debate
but there is no counter
to my opening statement
I like to love not liking things
I like being me
when love is what you have for me

Witness

Do I write, I'm not sure
there are three of us here
Is it you who inspires me?
or is it when I am with you
that I witness
and would put down
seems as if
these words
trace
our interface
the map
of our terrain

With you

I'll gladly
take damage
being with you
for I can
mend
but
if
the damage
is because of
you
I must decline
for this wound
is selfish
and
all mine

Phase-lock

I had to write you
a poem
not because
you're dope
or
to be
deep
far in
or profound
but because water
is life
god perhaps
it does something
when it's touching
the earth
It fills all
the spaces
saturates, steeps
ascends
and springs
running
phase-locked
with
expansive motion
then pressed
adjacent
as close as is possible
because I am earth
and you are
water

Too long

If you wait too long
you'll just be
a poem I wrote
a song I composed
I have the chords
the lyrics
I'm inspired
by what was
but
what will be
is my output
not ours
mine
if you wait too long
I'll be gone
not dead
just no longer for you
I love you
I would be tempted
if you rolled in
unexpected
I would burn down
the world
for you
but mine is already
rubble
I'm building it
back up
yet
I would rip out
the foundations
I painstakingly put down
I would
I would, I think
be
more than tempted
if you came back
unexpected

Map

If I were
to make a map
of myself
it wouldn't be of my
body
I'd forego all the parts
you already know
they preserved
Einstein's brain
in a jar
as if they could find
something special
in there
the map I would draw
a guide
to every place
the key
to the territory
of my soul
that you'll
never go

Break

Rolling in
then reflecting
reemitted
step up
step down
where would waves go
without constraint?
would they not ever
break
without a shoreline
does not any excitation
result from boundary
line
intersection
Where does the land
end
and the ocean begin?
Is the surface where
starts the sky?
maybe all things
are waves
that break
on their own shores

Turmoil

I was twenty
minutes
yesterday
up to my neck
seated on the gravel
near a waterfall
is was easy
to get in
but soon
turmoil
a rapid
yes
no
yes
I kept my hands above
the surface
like inverse gloves
it is an effort of will
I thought
but
noticed my focus
on calming
invited tremors
letting go though
of causal intent
broke the rhythm
the wanting
the fear of loss
are the same
come what may
I'm in

Uncharted

We fit
the signs
point them out
and I say
are valuable
it shows
love evolution
the pieces fit
meet
perfect
no border or start
or finish
justified
qualified
cut-out
whose criteria
nongeographical
boundaryless cartography
except, except
hold my hand now
in the fog
in the shadow
for the crossing
hold my hand
on the deck
at the helm
our vessel
at sea
where there be dragons

Space

The cement
the mortar
the glue
that connects me
to you
sentiments
delivered
not
idea substrate
but
reinforcement
independent
from what I say
there is no event
not time
or place
no upheaval
or uniformity
that permits
space
between you
and
me

Collection

Do you remember
when you first asked why
red dirt roads
high grass in the passing
not so distant trees
riding in the truck
cicadas
why
do you remember
curios eyes looking at it
before you were even seen
waking up to the folly
because of the wonder
and the beauty
asking why
is it broken
and no one will fix it
why
is it poisoned
and yet everyone drinks it
do you remember
why
you said no
why you had to go
do you remember the return
your fire collection
your focused intent
upon the correction
do you remember
your perfection
Do you remember your perfection?

Everyday

This day like any other
or as special as
any
day
is yours to claim
You do.
The way you walk
with purpose
but the way you look
with wonder
on this day
and
everyday
raises my spirit
to be witness
to your witnessing
touches my soul
I treasure it

Membrane

To you because
all is available
nothing is easy
everything is
the difference
indistinguishable
a mirror thin
membrane of thought
let it dissolve
release
let fly
let go
and
hit the mark

Surprise

A wave drew up
behind   me
and broke
on my back
the surprise of it
had me gasping
and sputtering
despite knowing
the nature of the shoreline
surprise me again
my love

How

How
I don't know the heart
I wait
turn back
and then
back again
paralyzed
balanced at
love
and
fear

Fleeting

If was was
never could be
infinity
at a point
a knifes edge
to be lost
floating
finding the dust
fleeting purchase
stepping from mote to mote
back to you

Anticipation

Walking in the dark
knowing the placement of things
lit by memory
familiar layout
extra sense navigation
intimate knowledge
no expectations
eager anticipation
and still
surprises

Edge

The present
moment is
not
a
sliver
not
an
instant
though it appears
to be
what seems
like an
edge
is a great
open field
surrender to
the now
for it is all
that is, was
and will be

Spool

All the words fail
all the gestures
nothing
the gold in the slate
iris
steel cable
inescapable
crossing is
a man on a wire
I
he
goes first
I am there
wait a little longer
while the tether spools
dust
are words
waving arms
and yet grace
besets
stillness
arrives
can you see me
in your eyes
I am there

Weft

Once there was a thread
now there is weaving
implicit loom
racked explicit
when you cross my mind

Singular

We met when I asked her
to dance
one hand in mine
the other on my shoulder
a singular moment
all eventualities
present
within seconds
materializing minutes
now
crystalized

List

I put you on my list
of all the things
the list is grand
grandiose
so, if one item is crossed off
all are
for if one thing on the list
is achieved
then every other item
must also have been
I put you on my list

More

There is more to this
I say
it works on many levels
all of them
a component that transcends
I say this and yet
the words are not the thing
what is the 'more'
to this?
more is the most
beyond
what a word
can do
we know 'it' at times
and remember knowing
though in the recollection
it is diminished
'there is more to this'
is enough
because
I know that you know
we never feel more
than when we are
together

Equinox

Night and day
spin up
spin down
equinox
touch paradox
ten thousand
thousand
miles
or
ten to the minus ten
I am inside
of you
and
you me
equidistant
duration
day and night

Ding

The noises
getting in the car
feel the rock
of the suspension
the clink of your keys
the pre-ignition
ding ding ding
door shut
chuckling
audio pick-up
spirit resonance
up or down
I hear you
in a millisecond
I feel you
profoundly subtle
instant input

Lost

Waves mock foundation
from a perspective
of certainty
frequency is the enemy
the rhythm of the real
It flows out and breaths in
but this
there is no loss
without the win
a firm position
affirmation
requires construction
constant attention
a cofferdam
hydrological fallacy
preventing the flood
at a cost
unwitting
fast holding to
the inevitable
lost time
surrender to the flow
the clock
love is thy rudder
rhythm the rock

Embers

What is inside you informs your bones, your eyes
your mind, your skin.

The rock embers of grief, of loss, injustice, a
smoking wall, but your light shines through it.
it blinds me
in the meeting
in the joinery

From inside, the light burns through the cracks.
I would see what is inside you, each hot stone
removed. Now I see.

Angelic heart

I am not afraid
I have to remind myself
love cannot be lost

golden electric
remembering the future
heart transmutation

a field of silver
bang bang maxwell's hammer
singular love strike

expect to preempt
cross the stream like as stone skip
space time wave function

the in between times
transition from to other
a blending of two

the mixture of two
timelines woven together
pick the thread that suites

resistance to one
desire for the other
investment in both

the outcome is blurred
there, responsibility
yes and no are one

what is all there is
one destiny for all things
free agent of love

golden threads twenty
strands fly away gossamer
tethered to my heart

a look lasting three
in your eyes minutes lifetimes
structural soundless

out to your heart reach
a precipice of feeling
love presentiment

the corporeal
tangent manifestation
skin of the spirit

location pinpoint
singularity of heart
awareness resides

informed by spirit
a sustained phase transition
body made of light

when you move light leaks
pulsing amber when you laugh
you speak indigo

findings linked jewels
things you had but didn't know
outside and inside

must a chain that binds
requires a lock and key
links that hold a clasp

gold the element
alchemical emerald
hold my hand a while

broken the old cart
fantasy axel sheared off
the wheels are still good

ethereal smoke
fragile connective tissue
reality test

the bed is well built
I would repair it with you
off road love wagon

essential pit-stop
a necessary pothole
suspension upgrade

the pendulum swings
in a well of gravity
approaching balance

is see your essence
we become what we behold
forever holding

hand in hand walking
water and sand firm surface
unless we linger

a thread couples us
entangled despite distance
orientation

channel cove ripples
witness each emanation
each beat of the heart

the waves will unify
propagate a confession
flame of resonance

hear a lake a heart
holds a singular nature
radiating fire

the bridge we construct
over the gulf an arrow
a causeway tethered

thread line rope cable
resolution amplitude
immeasurable

slack removed step once
intuitive transmission
we are back-to-back

letters for numbers
I will trade you a number
number for a word

phenetic is null
the number of love is all
give it a number

I could use the word
I prefer to add it up
the sum is the word

peripheral sight
reinforcement of the bond
connection pursuit

penumbra implied
in shadow light was conceived
blur perception

light suggests a source
no object emanates love
immaterial

there is no distance
faster than light between
touch resolution

a thousand moments
one to bifurcate a life
knit entanglement

halted precession
an instant eternity
shocking paradox

About the Author

Burch grew up in Taos, New Mexico. Originally the
land occupied by the native Pueblo Culture, the
Spanish colonized it, and hundreds of years later
it was the capital of the Territory of New Mexico
under the control of the United States. This
unique tri-cultural dynamic has influenced Burch
and his outlook from a young age. He has a degree
in Physics from UNM and an Industrial Design
degree from ArtCenter in Pasadena, California. His
interests are myriad, not the least of which is
the solution for a positive outcome for all. He is
a nerd, jock, philosopher, poet, and artist
spending a lot of time writing, creating content,
making jewelry, and designing products and product
systems.